INGLÉS PARA NIÑOS

READ ENGLISH WITH ZIGZAG -2

Copyright © 2022 Zigzag English / Lydia Winter

All rights reserved. No part of this publication may be reproduced or transmitted in any form without the written permission of the author.

ISBN: 978-1-914911-14-9

www.zigzagenglish.co.uk

OUR BOOKS FOR CHILDREN
www.zigzagenglish.co.uk

Our bilingual books for young children. Funny stories in simple, useful everyday English, with colour photos.
English with Tony -1- Tony moves house
English with Tony -2- Tony is happy
English with Tony -3- Tony's Christmas
English with Tony -4- Tony's holiday
My Best Friend

Our coursebook for child beginners (age 7 to 11)
English for Children - 1st Coursebook (Essential vocabulary and grammar for beginners)

Our series of dialogue books for beginners (for beginners aged 7 - 11). With word lists, comprehension questions, speaking tasks and more.
I Speak English Too! - 1
I Speak English Too! - 2

Our series of reading and comprehension books for beginners (for beginners aged 7 - 11). With word lists, comprehension questions and more.
Read English with Zigzag - 1
Read English with Zigzag - 2
Read English with Zigzag - 3
Read English with Zigzag 1, 2 and 3
    Audiobook - Books 1 + 2 (Audible)

The Learn English Activity Book for Children *(A1 - A2, elementary). (Recommended for children in early secondary school.)*

Our series of reading and comprehension books for children at elementary level (recommended for ages 10 - 13). With word lists, comprehension and discussion questions and lots of language activities.
Read English with Ben - 1
Read English with Ben - 2
Read English with Ben – 3

Our series of reading and discussion books (with writing tasks) for children at secondary school, A2 - B1
I Live in a Castle – Book 1 – The Choice
I Live in a Castle – Book 2 – The New Me

The Speak English, Read English, Write English Activity Books – *3 books from A1 to B2, for older children and adults.*

Our non-fiction book with language activities
Learn English with Fun Facts! – A2 – B2

English Dialogues for Secondary School – for ages 11 to 17, A2 – B2

OUR BOOKS FOR ADULTS

Our 3 Grammar books with grammar-focused dialogues
Learn English Grammar through Conversation – A1, A2 and B1

Our Dialogue books for adults (with vocabulary lists and comprehension questions)
50 very Easy Everyday English Dialogues (A2)
50 Easy Everyday English Dialogues (A2 - B1)
50 Intermediate Everyday English Dialogues (B1 - B2)
50 more Intermediate Everyday English Dialogues (B1 - B2)
40 Advanced Everyday English Dialogues (B2 – C1)
40 Intermediate Business English Dialogues (B1 - B2)
40 Advanced Business English Dialogues (B2 - C1)

Our activity books for adults and older children
The Speak English, Read English, Write English Activity Books – 3 books, for A1 - A2, A2 - B1 and B1 – B2.

Our non-fiction book with language activities
Learn English with Fun Facts! – A2 – B2

Contents

Los objetivos de esta serie de libros son: 5
Cómo utilizar esta serie de libros: 5
Qué más? ¿Y ahora qué? 5
1 I'm a tiger, remember? 7
2 What time is it? 10
3 A million bugs 11
4 How many animals are there? 13
5 Where is Poppy? 14
6 School uniform 16
7 I have an idea 17
8 School project 18
9 Be quiet 20
10 A quarter of an hour 21
11 I'm not scared 23
12 Picnic 24
13 A new plan 27
14 Book bag 28
15 Let me out! 30
16 Stripes and spots 31
17 YOWL! 32
18 Something strange 34
19 Not funny 35
20 The Headteacher 36
21 An exciting day 37
22 Sixty-one dogs and one spider 38
   Word Search 39
   Respuestas 40
Póngase en contacto con nosotros: 42
Sitio web: 42
Por favor... 42
   From: Read English with Zigzag - 3 43
   From: I Speak English Too! - 1 44
   From: The Learn English Activity Book 45

Los objetivos de esta serie de libros son:

1. Ofrecer una lectura divertida y amena.
2. Dotar a su hijo la confianza necesaria para leer en inglés.
3. Enseñar a su hijo palabras y frases clave. Los libros introducen, repiten y construyen sobre ellas poco a poco, para ampliar la comprensión del inglés de su hijo.
4. Ayudar a su hijo a aprender la gramática básica del inglés de forma sencilla.

Cómo utilizar esta serie de libros:

1. Tal vez su hijo disfrute leyendo los libros por su cuenta. ¡Estupendo! No obstante, si usted habla inglés, anímele a leer algunos capítulos en voz alta para ayudarle a mejorar su pronunciación. Hay disponible **un audiolibro de los dos primeros libros de Zigzag**.
2. Hay listas de vocabulario a lo largo de cada libro, que puede utilizar para ayudar a su hijo a aprender las palabras nuevas.
3. Encontrará preguntas de comprensión, con sus respectivas respuestas al final de cada libro. Por supuesto puede añadir más preguntas y conversar sobre la historia y los personajes.
4. Los libros incluyen actividades de aprendizaje para ayudar a su hijo con el vocabulario y la gramática.

Qué más? ¿Y ahora qué?

1. Nuestra serie de diálogos sencillos - I Speak English Too! - está pensada para aquellos padres que quieran ayudar a sus hijos a empezar a hablar inglés. Es ideal para que padres e hijos, o bien sólo los niños lean juntos. Empiece por lo más básico, introduciendo y ampliando las palabras y frases clave para ayudar a su hijo a progresar rápidamente. En pocas y divertidas lecciones, su hijo será capaz de mantener pequeñas conversaciones en inglés con usted.
2. La lectura de libros en inglés -por muy sencillos que sean- marca una gran diferencia. También recomendamos ver series de televisión sencillas para niños. Los audiolibros también son estupendos, sobre todo antes de acostarse (pues esto ayuda a retener el nuevo idioma). No espere que su hijo lo entienda todo en seguida: los audiolibros pueden escucharse una y otra vez, y su hijo entenderá más cada vez.

Cat or tiger?

1 I'm a tiger, remember?

Hello! I'm Zigzag. My name's Zigzag, and I'm a tiger. Yes, I'm a tiger.

No, I'm not a cat. I'm a tiger, remember?

Who are you? Are you a friend? I think you're my friend. Are you?

I live in this lovely house with my best friend, Pam. She's a dog, but I like her a lot. I'm big, but Pam is bigger. She's a very big, black and white dog.

Adam and Poppy live in my house too. They're not tigers or dogs, but they're okay. I quite like them. Sometimes they play with me. And sometimes they give me food.

What time is it? Oh! It's **dinner** time!

Poppy – WHERE'S MY CAT FOOD? GIVE ME MY CAT FOOD!

Vocabulary
- to remember   recordar
- dinner   cena

2 What time is it?

It's half past twelve.
It's 12:30.

It's seven o'clock in the morning.
It's 7:00 AM.

It's ten to six.
It's 5:50.

It's five past five in the afternoon.
It's 5:05 PM.

It's a quarter to four.
It's 3:45.

3 A million bugs

Hello again! Today, I want to **show** you my garden. Pam wants to show you the garden too. But it's not Pam's garden, it's my garden. Can Pam come too? Yes, she can come if she wants.

My garden has two **trees**. My garden has lots of **flowers**. But the best thing about my garden is the **bugs**. How many bugs are there in my garden? There are a million bugs!

What's my favourite bug? Can you **guess**? I think you can.

I like **bees** and butterflies. But I love spiders. Butterflies are beautiful and bees are intelligent. But spiders are **delicious**.

Vocabulary
- to show — mostrar
- tree — árbol
- flower — flor
- bug — bicho, insecto
- to guess — adivinar
- bee — abeja
- delicious — delicioso

4 How many animals are there?

There are three animals.

How many people are there?

There is one person.

How many children are there?
There's one child.

5 Where is Poppy?

Hi there!

Can I ask you a question?

Where is Poppy? Why isn't she here? Where does she go every day?

Is she hiding in the house?

Is she outside, in the garden?

Do you know where she is?

I'm looking for Poppy. I'm looking for her **downstairs**, in the living-room and the kitchen. And I'm looking for her upstairs, in the bedrooms and the bathroom.

I'm looking for her **inside**, and I'm looking for her outside.

But I can't **find** her. Why not? Please **help** me find her!

Vocabulary
- to ask a question   hacer una pregunta
- downstairs   abajo
- inside   dentro
- to find   encontrar a
- to help   ayudar

6 School uniform

It's Monday today and it's a quarter to nine. So Poppy's walking to school with her school friend Jessica and with Jessica's mum.

What does Jessica look like? Does she look like Poppy? No, she doesn't. Poppy has **long** brown hair and brown eyes. But Jessica has **short fair** hair and blue eyes. She's **taller** than Poppy.

In England, children have to wear **school uniform**. Poppy and Jessica's uniform is black **trousers** and a red top.

The girls are a bit **late** to school today. They have to run. They get to school at 9 o'clock. **Just in time.**

Questions:
1. Who is shorter, Jessica or Poppy?
2. Why do the children have to run?
3. Why are they **wearing the same** clothes?

Vocabulary:
- long — largo
- short — corto
- fair — rubio
- tall — alto
- school uniform — uniforme escolar
- trousers — pantalones
- late — tarde
- just in time — justo a tiempo
- to wear — llevar
- same — mismo

7 I have an idea

Hello everybody!

I have a problem. I **STILL** can't find Poppy.

She's not in the house – upstairs or downstairs. And she's not in the garden.

I don't know where she is. You don't know where she is. Pam doesn't know where she is.

Nobody knows where she is!

Luckily, I have an idea.

Do you want to know what my idea is?

Guess!

Vocabulary:
- still   todavía
- luckily   por suerte

8 School project

Poppy is doing a project at school. She has to ask all the children in her class about their pets. She has to **find out** what her class's favourite pet is.

Poppy **draws** a **graph**:

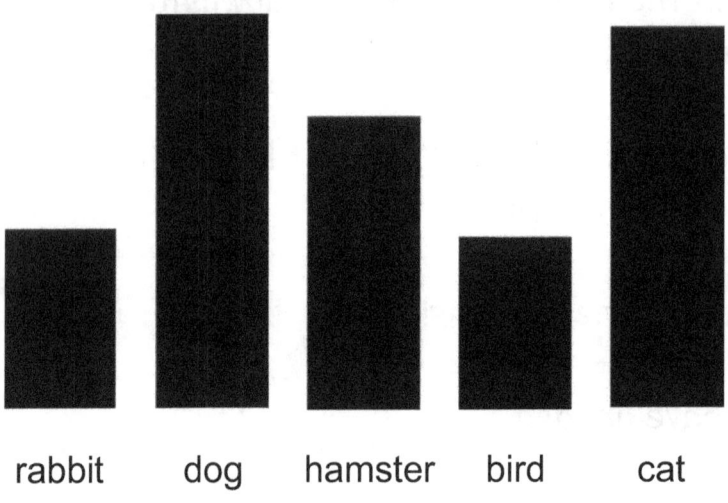

rabbit   dog   hamster   bird   cat

The dog is the most **popular** pet. Lots of children have dogs, but cats are very popular too. Rabbits and birds are the **least** popular pets.

Nobody has a snake or a spider. And nobody has a **lion** or a tiger.

Questions:
1. **Which** pet is the most popular?
2. Which is the least popular?
3. How many children have pet snakes?

Vocabulary:
- project — proyecto
- to find out — saber
- to draw — dibujar
- graph — gráfico
- least — menos
- lion — león
- which — que

9 Be quiet

Shhh...

Be quiet.

Be very, very quiet.

I don't want Poppy to **hear** me. I don't want Poppy to see me. I don't want Poppy to know I'm here.

Poppy's wearing her black trousers and her red top again.

Poppy's **opening** the **door**. Poppy's going outside.

I'm going outside too! I'm going with Poppy.

Today is the day I find out where Poppy goes every day.

Do you want to come too?

Vocabulary:
- to hear   escuchar
- to open   abrir
- door   puerta

10 A quarter of an hour

Poppy and Jessica are going to school again today. Walking to school takes them fifteen minutes – a **quarter** of an hour.

First they turn left. Then they turn right. Then they cross the **main road** at the **zebra crossing**.

Some children go to school by car and some go by **bike**. But most children walk to school with their mum or dad.

There are lots of children and parents **in front of** the school. They're **waiting** for the school to open. Jessica and Poppy are early for school today.

Questions:
1. How long does it take Jessica and Poppy to walk to school?
2. Do all the children at their school walk to school?
3. Why are there so many people outside the school?

Vocabulary:
- quarter — cuarto
- main road — carretera principal
- zebra crossing — paso de cebra
- bike — bicicleta
- in front of — frente a
- to wait — esperar

11 I'm not scared

Are you there? Are you coming with me?

Be **careful**! Be careful of the cars!

Quick – **cross** the road now!

Where's Poppy? There she is. She's with Jessica.

But who are all the **other** people? There are so **many** people here. And so many cars and bikes.

Are you **scared**? Don't be scared.

I'm not scared. I'm **never** scared.

WHAT'S THAT?! IS IT A VERY BIG DOG?!

RUN!!

Vocabulary:
- careful — cuidado
- quick — rápido
- to cross — cruzar
- other — otros
- so many people — tanta gente
- scared — asustado
- never — nunca

12 Picnic

This weekend, Poppy and Adam's family is going on a picnic by the **river**.

The picnic is delicious. There are chicken sandwiches, cheese and **ham** sandwiches, little tomatoes, **strawberries** and **lemon cake**. There's **orange juice** to drink. There's dog food for Pam.

It's a beautiful day. It's **sunny** but not too hot.

Mum and dad are tired. They go to sleep.

Poppy **reads** her **boo**k. She's reading about tigers in India. It's very **interesting**. Poppy really likes tigers.

Suddenly, she hears Adam **shouting** – "HELP!" He's **falling** into the river!

Poppy runs. But Pam runs **faster**. She **jumps** into the **water**. She helps Adam. He's **safe** now.

That was **scary**.

Well done, Pam. Good dog!

Questions:
1. Where are Poppy's family having a picnic?
2. Why do mum and dad go to sleep?
3. What happens to Adam?

Vocabulary:
- river — rio
- ham — jamón
- strawberry — fresa
- lemon cake — pastel de limón
- orange juice — zumo de naranja
- sunny — soleado
- to read — leer
- book — libro
- interesting — interesante
- suddenly — de repente
- to shout — gritar
- to fall — caer
- faster — más rápido
- to jump — saltar
- water — agua
- safe — seguro
- scary — aterrador
- well done — bien hecho

:

13 A new plan

Hello! Remember – be quiet! Shhh...

Yes, I'm trying again today.

I have a new idea. I have a new plan.

Look over there. Look at Poppy's bag. Look at her red **book bag.**

How many books are there in Poppy's bag? Is there one book in the bag? Are there two books in the bag? Or are there no books in the bag?

There are no books in the bag.

No books, but one cat.

Vocabulary:
- book bag   bolsa de libros / mochilla escolar

14 Book bag

Poppy's walking to school. She walks to school every day. She walks to school on Monday, Tuesday, Wednesday, Thursday and Friday.

But today, something is different. Poppy's bag is **heavy**.

Her bag is often heavy. It's a book bag – a bag for books – and books are heavy.

But today the bag is really heavy. **Extremely** heavy.

Something else is different, too.

Today, Poppy's bag is **moving**.

Is there something in the bag? Is it a book? Or - is it something else?

Questions:
1. What kind of bag does Poppy have?
2. Why is her bag so heavy today?
3. How heavy is the bag?

Vocabulary:
- heavy — pesado
- extremely — extremadamente
- something else — otra cosa
- to move — moverse

15 Let me out!

Are you there? Can you hear me?

You can't see me, because I'm in Poppy's book bag.

It's very **uncomfortable** in here. I'm big, and the bag is small. The bag is too small for a tiger.

I'm hot and **thirsty**.

I want **to get out**.

I can't get out! I'm **stuck**! I'm stuck in this horrible bag!

I **hate** this bag. I hate it, hate it, hate it, HATE it!

Poppy! Let me out!

POPPY!!

Vocabulary:
- uncomfortable   incómodo
- I'm thirsty   tengo sed
- to get out   salir
- stuck   atascado
- to hate   odiar

16 Stripes and spots

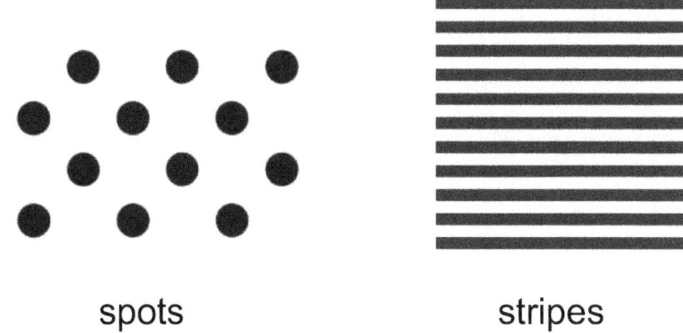

spots   stripes

Who do these stripes and spots belong to?

1

2

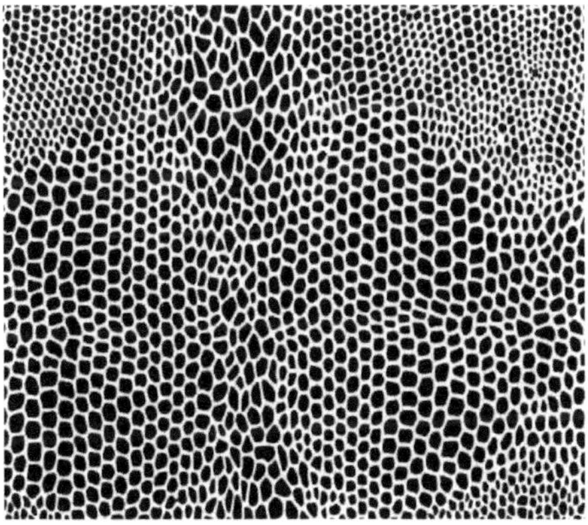

3

4

17 YOWL!

BUMP! THAT HURT!

Poppy's opening the bag now. I can get out of the bag.

3, 2, 1 and OUT!

AT LAST! YOWL, YOWL, YOWL, YOWL! I'M OUT OF THE BAG!

RUN! RUN!

Look at all the children. There are lots and lots of children here. There are 5, 10, 15, 20, 25 children! That's too many children.

Hello children. I'm Zigzag. I'm a tiger. I'm a nice, friendly tiger. Are you nice, friendly children?

Oh no. Why are people shouting? Why are they shouting at me?

Why is Poppy **picking me up**? Why is she **putting me back** in the horrible bag?

Let me out!

Vocabulary:
- to pick up   coger
- to put back   colocar de nuevo

18 Something strange

Today, when Poppy and Jessica get to school, something **strange** happens.

Poppy goes into her **classroom** and says hello to her friends. The teacher, Mrs Rice, tells the children to sit down. She gives them **work** to do. Poppy needs a book. She opens her book bag.

And then…

Something jumps out of the bag. Something big. It makes a very strange noise. Then it runs **round** the classroom. It runs very fast. Three times round the room. Children are **screaming** and climbing onto chairs. Mrs Rice is shouting. "Stop it!" she shouts. "Everyone sit down! Poppy, take that cat home. Now."

Questions:
1. Why does Poppy open her book bag?
2. How many times does Zigzag run round the room?
3. What does the teacher tell Poppy to do?

Vocabulary:
- strange — extraño
- classroom — aula
- work — trabajo
- round — alrededor
- to scream — gritar

19 Not funny

It's you again, is it? Okay.

Why are you looking at me? Are you **laughing** at me? Stop laughing. It's not **funny**.

Yes, I'm back home. Yes, Poppy and her mum and dad are angry with me.

Why are they angry? I don't understand. It's not my fault. It's all Poppy's fault.

I don't like Poppy. I don't like her mum and dad. I don't like this house.

I'm going outside. I want to hide from all the people. I want to hide from Pam, and I want to hide from you.

Please **leave me alone** now.

Vocabulary:
- to laugh — reírse
- funny — divertido
- to leave alone — dejar en paz

20 The Headteacher

Poppy's **in trouble**. Cats aren't **allowed** in the classroom. Why was Zigzag in Poppy's bag? Poppy says it's Zigzag's fault, but the teacher doesn't **believe** her. She thinks it's Poppy's fault.

Poppy has to **talk** to the Headteacher. She **tells** her about Zigzag and the book bag. She says sorry.

The Headteacher **smiles**. The Headteacher laughs. The Headteacher has an idea.

It's a great idea. Poppy's very happy. All the children are excited.

I can't wait to tell Zigzag, thinks Poppy.

Questions:
1. Who is angry about Zigzag coming to school?
2. Who thinks it's funny?
3. What do you think the Headteacher's idea is?

Vocabulary:
- in trouble — en problemas
- allowed — permitido
- to believe — creer
- to talk — hablar
- to tell — decir a
- to smile — sonreír

21 An exciting day

Hi! It's great to see you!

Today is an **exciting** day. A very exciting day. I'm so excited!

I'm going to school with Poppy today. Yes, that's right, I'm going to school with Poppy again.

This time, Poppy WANTS me to go to school with her.

I'm not going to school in Poppy's book bag. No, this time I'm going to school in my cat **basket**.

Look at me in my beautiful cat basket! Look at me, everyone!

And look at Pam – she's coming too.

There are lots of cats and dogs at school today.

Poppy – can I go to school with you every day?

Vocabulary:
- exciting   emocionante
- basket   cesta

22 Sixty-one dogs and one spider

Today is the day when pets can come to school.

Yes, the Headteacher's idea is that today, and only today, all the children can bring their pets to school.

There are 61 dogs. There are 53 cats. There are 17 hamsters. There are 8 rabbits. There are 5 birds. There are 3 rats. There are 2 snakes. There is 1 spider.

I hope the dogs don't chase the cats and the rabbits. I hope the cats don't eat the birds and the hamsters. I hope the rats, the snakes and the spider stay in their cages.

It's a scary day. But it's a good day too.

Can you read these numbers?
61 = sixty-one
53 = fifty-three
17 = seventeen

How about these numbers?
2782 = two thousand, seven hundred and eighty-two
90,511 = ninety thousand, five hundred and eleven

Word Search

```
J F A F G H A D S W K D U E X
Y P L L U G C C N A D H W N A
S B Q Y E O P C H D L D P U S
J Y R J S T P Z F E H A A F U
L V F X S X L M C L A V U F F
P V R D H V L T H I R S T Y K
S O I S U N G I O C V K A Q T
P O P U L A R R R I V E R U E
F U N N Y G L E M O N C O F E
H T P N I D X D D U N A E O E
S S E Y T K S G W S C J E Y H
Q I U D L L K O P P B Q E B V
K D L L Q A G K H G I M A I K
M E X T R E M E L Y Z F L K W
A J H S J U S C P P Y O R E N
```

- It's a hot, **su_n_** day. I want to have a picnic **o_ts_de** by the **ri_e_**. We can go swimming.
- It's too hot! Adam's **ex_r_mely t_red** and **th_r_ty**. He drinks lots of water and goes to bed.
- What are Poppy and Adam like? Poppy is **pop_l_r** – she has lots of friends. Adam is **f_n_y**. He makes me laugh!
- Do you walk to school, or do you go by **b_k_**?
- This ◯ cake is **deli_i_u_**!
- How old are you? - **Gu_ss**!

39

Respuestas

1. Poppy is shorter.
2. Because they're late to school.
3. Because they're wearing school uniform.

8

1. The dog is the most popular.
2. The bird is the least popular.
3. No children have snakes.

10

1. It takes them fifteen minutes (a quarter of an hour) to walk to school.
2. No, some go to school by car or bike.
3. Because they're waiting for the school to open.

12

1. They're having a picnic by the river.
2. Because they're tired.
3. He falls into the river.

14

1. She has a book bag.
2. Because there's a cat in it.
3. It's extremely heavy.

16

1. A zebra.
2. A dalmatian dog.
3. A snake.
4. A leopard.

18
1. Because she needs a book.
2. He runs round the room three times.
3. She tells her to take her cat home.

20
1. Poppy's teacher is angry.
2. The Headteacher thinks it's funny.

Gracias por leer este libro.

Póngase en contacto con nosotros:

Esperamos que usted y su hijo hayan encontrado este libro útil.

Si tiene alguna pregunta sobre este libro, envíenosla y nos pondremos en contacto con usted lo antes posible. Si tiene alguna sugerencia para la próxima edición de este libro, o para otros libros que le gustaría que publicáramos para ayudar a su hijo a aprender inglés, nos encantaría escucharla.

Escríbanos a: lydiawinter.zigzagenglish@gmail.com

Sitio web:

Puede echar un vistazo a nuestros otros libros para niños y adultos, jugar a algunos juegos en inglés y leer nuestro blog, en: **www.zigzagenglish.co.uk**.

Por favor...

...escribe una reseña sobre este libro. Las reseñas son importantes para otros padres y también para nosotros. Gracias.

From: Read English with Zigzag - 3

11 Cat in a tree

The white cat sat in the tree. It sat in the tree for five long minutes.

I wanted that cat. I don't know why I wanted her, but I did.

Zigzag is a cat, and I don't chase Zigzag. But Zigzag is family. I chase every other cat. All dogs chase cats. It's what we do.

But I had a problem. Cats can **climb** trees. Dogs can't climb trees. The white cat was in a tree. I needed to go **up**, or I needed the cat to come **down**.

I tried to climb the tree. I really, really **tried**. But it was no good. I'm big, strong, brave and intelligent, but I can't climb.

I **asked** the cat to come down. I said I wanted to talk to her. I was very **polite**. She was polite too, but she said no. She didn't want to come down. She was comfortable in the tree. It was nice up there.

I wanted that cat.

From: I Speak English Too! - 1

10B

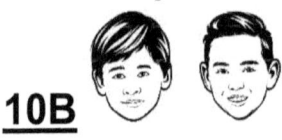

Sam: Do you like **shopping**, Jack?

Jack: Yes, I love shopping. I like **buying** new **clothes** with my mum.

Sam: **How often** do you buy new clothes?

Jack: Quite often. Maybe **once a month**.

Sam: I like new clothes too. But my mum says they're too **expensive**.

Jack: Some clothes shops are **cheap**. And buying online is cheap too.

Sam: I really want some new **trainers**. But the ones I like are very expensive.

Jack: Maybe **wait** till **Christmas**?

Sam: What do you want for Christmas?

Jack: I want a new **jacke**t. A beautiful red one. It's online.

Sam: Is it cheap?

Jack: No, not really. But it's for Christmas!

From: The Learn English Activity Book

MARK'S HOLIDAYS – True or False?

My name's Mark. There are five of us in my family – my parents, my older sister, my little brother and me. We live in a big, noisy **modern** city. My parents work very hard at work and my sister and I work very hard at school. So we love going on holiday!

My family goes on holiday once or twice a year. We usually go in the summer, in August, because that's when the long school holidays are. And sometimes we go away at Christmas too, to stay with my grandparents in their big house in a different, nicer city.

I like going on holiday in the summer because it's hot. We often go to the seaside and it's warm enough to swim in the sea. But my mum doesn't really like going to the beach. She says it's too hot and too boring. She likes staying in old hotels in beautiful towns and cities. She loves good food and she wants to eat at a different restaurant every evening. My little brother is only three. He's not interested in restaurants. He usually wants to go to the park to play on the swings. My sister is sixteen now. She says she wants to go on holiday with her friends next year. My dad always has fun on holiday. He's happy not to be at work!

1. Mark is the youngest child in his family. **T / F**
2. His parents both like their jobs. **T / F**
3. They go on holiday every year. **T / F**
4. They all like doing the **same** things on holiday. **T / F**
5. Mark's grandparents don't live in the **countryside**. **T / F**
6. Mark's sister is lazy. **T / F**
7. Mark loves his city. **T / F**
8. Mark's mum doesn't want to go to the beach every summer. **T / F**
9. Everyone likes hot weather! **T / F**
10. Mark stays with his grandparents in their flat once a year. **T / F**

www.ingramcontent.com/pod-product-compliance
Lightning Source LLC
LaVergne TN
LVHW051206080426
835508LV00021B/2831